THE PSYCHOLOGY OF MONEY, GROWTH AND WEALTH

The Best Way to Change the World

IJIGBAN DANIEL OKETA

Copyright

All Rights Reserved 2024 @ Ijigban Daniel Oketa.

THE PSYCHOLOGY OF MONEY, GROWTH AND WEALTH

ISBN: 9798329016406

No part of this publication may be reproduced, distributed, or transmitted in any form or by any means, including photocopying, recording, or other electronic or mechanical methods, without the prior written permission of the author and copyright holder, except in the case of brief quotations embodied in critical reviews and certain other noncommercial uses permitted by copyright law.

For permissions requests or inquiries, please contact.

+234 703-738-4814
oketadaniels@gmail.com

Contents

PREFACE 4

CHAPTER 1: THE SPIRITUALITY OF MONEY 7

CHAPTER 2: MONEY MISTAKES MOST PEOPLE MAKE 13

CHAPTER 3: REVOLUTIONARY MONEY MINDSET 19

CHAPTER 4: THE CREATOR ECONOMY 25

CHAPTER 5: SECRETS OF SUSTAINABLE WEALTH 31

CHAPTER 6: TRANSFORMATIVE LEADERSHIP AND CHANGE 37

CHAPTER 7: INSPIRING STORIES OF FINANCIAL EMPOWERMENT . 43

CONCLUSION: EMBRACING COMPREHENSIVE FINANCIAL AND PERSONAL GROWTH 51

PREFACE

In "The Psychology of Money, Growth, and Wealth," you embark on an enlightening journey to unravel the complex relationships and perceptions that define our financial behaviors and influence our economic success.

This compelling narrative not only dives deep into the economic and psychological aspects of money but also explores its spiritual dimensions, providing a comprehensive exploration of what truly drives our financial decisions and the consequences thereof.

The Spirituality of Money: This section delves into the often-overlooked spiritual aspect of money and the spirituality of making money, examining how our financial life reflects our inner values and spiritual beliefs. It explores the idea that money, much like energy, should be a force for good or ill, depending on how it is channeled, emphasizing the need for alignment between our spiritual position and financial goals.

Money Mistakes Most People Make: Here, the book highlights common financial pitfalls that individuals from various walks of life encounter. From the failure to understand the true value of money to the traps of consumerism, it discusses how these mistakes can be avoided by fostering greater awareness and adopting a more mindful approach to spending and saving.

Revolutionary Money Mindset "Revolutionary Money Mindset" shifts your mind from traditional views on wealth accumulation to innovative and transformative strategies that promise not just financial growth but also personal fulfillment. This chapter challenges everyone to redefine success and reconfigure their financial strategies to support a life that is rich not only in material terms but in purpose and satisfaction.

The Creator Economy: Focusing on the burgeoning creator economy, this section examines how digital platforms have democratized the means of production and distribution, enabling more individuals to turn their passions into profit. It discusses how leveraging creativity and innovation within this economy can lead to unprecedented financial independence and growth.

Secret of Sustainable Wealth: the book uncovers the principles behind building and maintaining or transferring wealth over the long term. It argues that sustainable wealth is not solely about accumulation but also about the wise management and ethical stewardship of resources. This chapter provides practical advice on creating systems that ensure wealth can be a source of lasting security and a legacy for future generations.

Transformative Leadership and Change: Adding a crucial dimension to the discourse, this section addresses the role of universal leadership purpose of humanity and shaping financial destinies. It argues that true leadership involves guiding not just oneself but also others towards financial enlightenment and empowerment, advocating for transformative change that aligns personal success with broader societal benefits.

"The Psychology of Money, Growth, and Wealth" is an essential read for anyone looking to transform their financial life comprehensively. It offers a unique blend of spiritual insight, practical advice, and psychological acumen tailored for anyone aspiring to redefine their relationship with money and embark on a true path to wealth and personal growth.

Yours Success-Friend,
Ijigban Daniel Oketa.

Chapter 1: The Spirituality of Money

Money, often regarded purely as a means of transaction, holds much deeper significance. Beyond its materialistic essence, money interacts intricately with our inner values, spiritual beliefs, and personal philosophies.

Understanding this spiritual dimension of money can transform our financial behavior and lead to a more fulfilling and ethical approach to wealth.

1.1 Understanding the Spiritual Dimension of Money

The Connection between Money and Inner Values

Money, at its core, is a reflection of our values and priorities. It serves as a mirror, revealing what we truly care about. For instance, someone who prioritizes family may allocate a significant portion of their income to household expenses and children's education. Conversely, a person driven by status might spend more on luxury items and social events.

Our inner values shape our financial decisions, whether consciously or unconsciously. When we spend money, we are essentially making choices about what we deem important. This connection between money and values underscores the need for self-awareness in financial management. By understanding our core values, we can align our spending habits and financial goals with what truly matters to us, leading to more intentional and satisfying financial behavior.

Spiritual Beliefs and Financial Behavior

Spiritual beliefs profoundly influence how we perceive and manage money. Different spiritual traditions offer varied perspectives on wealth and financial behavior. For example, many Eastern philosophies, such as Buddhism and Hinduism, emphasize detachment from material wealth and promote simplicity and contentment. These teachings encourage individuals to seek fulfillment beyond material possessions and to use money as a tool for supporting spiritual growth and community well-being.

In contrast, certain interpretations of Western religious traditions, like Christianity, suggest that wealth is a blessing but also emphasize the importance of charity, stewardship, and ethical conduct. The concept of tithing, or giving a portion of one's income to the church or charity, reflects the belief that money should be used to support communal and spiritual causes.

These spiritual perspectives shape financial behavior by providing ethical guidelines and promoting a mindset of abundance, generosity, and responsibility. Understanding how spiritual beliefs influence our financial decisions can help us cultivate a more balanced and ethical approach to money management.

1.2 Money as Energy:

The Concept of Money as a Force for Good or Ill

Money, much like energy, has the potential to create positive or negative outcomes based on how it is utilized. This perspective frames money not merely as a static resource but as a dynamic force that can influence our lives and the world around us.

When channeled positively, money can become a powerful tool for good. It can fund education, healthcare, and community development projects, significantly improving the quality of life for many. Philanthropy and charitable giving are prime examples of how money can be used to support societal well-being and promote social justice.

On the other hand, money can also be a source of harm when misused. Greed, corruption, and exploitation often arise from the pursuit of wealth at the expense of ethical considerations. The negative impact of such behavior can be seen in various societal issues, including income inequality, environmental degradation, and financial crises.

Recognizing money as a form of energy helps us understand the importance of our intentions and actions in financial matters. It prompts us to reflect on how our financial choices can contribute to or detract from the greater good.

Channeling Money Positively

Channeling money positively requires intentionality and mindfulness in our financial practices. Here are some strategies to help align our financial behavior with positive outcomes:

1. **Mindful Spending:** Be conscious of where and how you spend your money. Choose to support businesses and causes that align with your values. For instance, purchasing from companies that practice ethical sourcing and environmental sustainability can contribute to positive change.

2. **Philanthropy and Charity:** Allocate a portion of your income to charitable organizations and community projects. This not only supports those in need but also fosters a sense of purpose and connection.

3. **Investing in Social Good:** Consider impact investing, where you invest in businesses and projects that generate social and environmental benefits alongside financial returns. This approach allows your money to work towards positive change.

4. **Financial Education:** Equip yourself and others with financial literacy. Understanding how to manage money effectively can prevent financial hardships and empower individuals to make informed decisions.

5. **Ethical Business Practices:** If you are a business owner or entrepreneur, prioritize ethical practices in your operations. This includes fair wages, sustainable sourcing, and transparent dealings, contributing to a more equitable and responsible business environment.

By adopting these practices, we can ensure that our financial behavior reflects our spiritual values and contributes to the well-being of society. Channeling money positively transforms it from a mere transactional tool into a force for good, fostering a sense of fulfillment and alignment with our higher values.

Conclusion

The spirituality of money invites us to look beyond the surface of financial transactions and explore the deeper connections between our inner values, spiritual beliefs, and financial behavior. Understanding money as a form of energy that can be channeled for good or ill empowers us to make more mindful and intentional financial decisions. By aligning our financial practices with our spiritual values, we can create a more fulfilling and ethical approach to wealth, contributing to both personal growth and societal well-being.

Chapter 2: Money Mistakes Most People Make

In the journey towards financial stability and growth, many individuals encounter common pitfalls that can hinder their progress. This chapter aims to highlight these mistakes, provide insights into their underlying causes, and offer practical strategies to avoid them.

2.1 Misunderstanding the True Value of Money

The Illusion of Wealth

One of the most pervasive misconceptions about money is equating it with wealth. Many people believe that accumulating money or material possessions is the ultimate measure of success and security. This illusion often leads to a relentless pursuit of more—more money, more assets, more luxury—without understanding what true wealth entails.

The illusion of wealth can create a cycle of dissatisfaction, where no amount of money feels sufficient. This is because real wealth is not solely about financial accumulation; it encompasses security, freedom, peace of mind, and the ability to live a fulfilling life. Understanding that wealth is multi-dimensional helps shift the focus from mere accumulation to achieving a balanced and meaningful financial life.

Re-evaluating What Money Means

To move beyond the illusion of wealth, it's crucial to re-evaluate our perceptions of money. Money should be seen as a tool to facilitate our goals and improve our quality of life rather than an end in itself. Here are some ways to reframe our understanding of money:

1. **Purposeful Financial Goals:** Define what financial success means to you personally. This could include financial security, the ability to support loved ones, or the freedom to pursue passions and hobbies.

2. **Quality Over Quantity:** Focus on experiences and relationships that bring joy and satisfaction, rather than accumulating material goods.

3. **Financial Freedom:** Aim for financial independence, which allows you to make choices based on what you value most, rather than being constrained by financial pressures.

By redefining money's role in our lives, we can create a healthier relationship with it, one that supports our overall well-being and happiness.

2.2 The Traps of Consumerism

Recognizing Consumerist Pitfalls

Consumerism is deeply ingrained in modern society, often driven by advertising and social pressure to own the latest and greatest products. This relentless focus on consumption can lead to several pitfalls, including:

1. **Debt Accumulation:** Spending beyond one's means often results in significant debt, which can become a heavy financial burden.

2. **Lack of Savings:** Prioritizing immediate gratification over long-term financial health can lead to insufficient savings and investment for the future.

3. **Emotional Spending:** Using shopping as a way to cope with stress or emotions can lead to impulsive purchases and financial regret.

Recognizing these consumerist pitfalls is the first step towards overcoming them. It involves being mindful of how advertising and societal norms influence our spending habits and making conscious decisions that align with our true needs and values.

Overcoming Materialistic Tendencies

Overcoming materialistic tendencies requires a shift in mindset and behavior. Here are some strategies to help:

1. **Mindful Consumption:** Before making a purchase, consider whether it aligns with your values and needs. Ask yourself if it will add lasting value to your life.

2. **Decluttering:** Regularly assess your possessions and remove items that no longer serve a purpose. This practice can help you appreciate what you have and resist the urge to accumulate more.

3. **Setting Financial Priorities:** Focus on spending money on experiences and activities that bring long-term satisfaction rather than short-term gratification.

4. **Emotional Awareness:** Recognize emotional triggers that lead to impulsive spending and find healthier ways to cope, such as exercise, meditation, or talking to a friend.

By adopting these practices, you can reduce materialistic tendencies and foster a more mindful approach to consumption, leading to better financial health and overall satisfaction.

2.3 Fostering Financial Awareness

Developing a Mindful Approach to Spending

Mindful spending involves being aware of your financial habits and making intentional choices about how you use your money. This practice can help prevent unnecessary expenditures and ensure that your spending aligns with your values and goals. Here's how to develop a mindful approach to spending:

1. **Track Your Expenses:** Keep a record of all your expenses to understand where your money is going. This can help identify areas where you can cut back.

2. **Create a Budget:** Establish a budget that reflects your financial goals and stick to it. This ensures that you're spending within your means and prioritizing savings.

3. **Evaluate Purchases:** Before making a purchase, consider if it's a need or a want. Delay gratification by waiting a few days before buying to see if the desire persists.

Practical Tips for Conscious Saving

Conscious saving involves making deliberate choices to set aside money for future needs and goals. Here are some practical tips to help you save more effectively:

1. **Automate Savings:** Set up automatic transfers to your savings account to ensure you save consistently without having to think about it.

2. **Set Clear Goals:** Define specific savings goals, such as an emergency fund, a vacation, or retirement. Having clear goals can motivate you to save.

3. **Reduce Unnecessary Expenses:** Identify non-essential expenses that you can cut back on, such as dining out, subscriptions, or impulse purchases.

4. **Increase Income:** Look for ways to boost your income, such as taking on a side job or freelance work, to increase your savings potential.

5. **Emergency Fund:** Build an emergency fund that covers at least three to six months' worth of living expenses. This provides a financial cushion in case of unexpected events.

By fostering financial awareness and adopting mindful spending and saving habits, you can avoid common money mistakes and build a more secure and fulfilling financial future.

Chapter 3: Revolutionary Money Mindset

In today's rapidly evolving financial landscape, adopting a revolutionary mindset towards money is essential for achieving lasting wealth and personal fulfillment. This chapter explores how shifting perspectives on wealth accumulation, embracing innovative financial strategies, and redefining success can transform your financial journey.

3.1 Shifting Perspectives on Wealth Accumulation

Moving Beyond Traditional Views

Traditionally, wealth accumulation has been viewed through a narrow lens focused primarily on earning, saving, and investing. While these fundamentals remain important, a revolutionary money mindset involves expanding this perspective to include personal fulfillment, social impact, and overall life satisfaction.

- **Holistic Financial Health:** Understanding that wealth is not just about money but includes emotional well-being, physical health, and strong relationships.

- **Financial Resilience:** Developing a mindset that embraces adaptability and resilience in the face of economic changes and uncertainties.

- **Purpose-Driven Wealth:** Aligning your financial activities with your broader life purpose and values, ensuring that your wealth-building efforts contribute to your overall happiness and well-being.

Embracing New Financial Strategies

A revolutionary approach to money also involves embracing new financial strategies that leverage modern tools and technologies.

- **Digital Assets and Cryptocurrencies:** Exploring opportunities in digital currencies and blockchain technology, which offer new avenues for investment and wealth creation.

- **Sustainable and Ethical Investing:** Investing in companies and projects that align with your values and contribute positively to society and the environment.

- **Gig Economy and Freelancing:** Leveraging the flexibility and opportunities offered by the gig economy to diversify income streams and achieve financial independence.

3.2 Innovative and Transformative Financial Strategies

Techniques for Financial Growth

Implementing innovative and transformative financial strategies is crucial for maximizing financial growth. Here are some key techniques:

- **Passive Income Streams:** Building multiple sources of passive income, such as real estate investments, dividend-paying stocks, and digital products, to create a steady cash flow with minimal ongoing effort.

- **Automated Investing:** Using robo-advisors and automated investing platforms to manage and grow your investments efficiently and cost-effectively.

- **Leveraging Technology:** Utilizing financial apps and tools to track expenses, manage budgets, and optimize investment portfolios.

Balancing Material Wealth with Personal Fulfillment

True financial success goes beyond material wealth; it also involves achieving personal fulfillment and living a meaningful life. Balancing these aspects requires a conscious effort to align financial goals with personal values and aspirations.

- **Experiential Spending:** Prioritizing spending on experiences, such as travel and personal development, over material possessions, as experiences often provide more lasting happiness and fulfillment.

- **Philanthropy and Giving Back:** Integrating charitable giving and community involvement into your financial plan to create a positive impact and enhance your sense of purpose.

- **Work-Life Balance:** Striving for a balance between work and personal life to ensure that financial pursuits do not come at the expense of health, relationships, and overall well-being.

3.3 Redefining Success

Understanding True Wealth

Redefining success involves understanding that true wealth encompasses more than just financial assets. It includes:

- **Time Freedom:** Having the flexibility to spend your time as you choose, pursuing passions and interests without being constrained by financial pressures.

- **Health and Well-Being:** Prioritizing physical and mental health, as well as maintaining a supportive social network.

- **Legacy and Impact:** Creating a lasting legacy through meaningful contributions to family, community, and society.

Aligning Financial Goals with Life Purpose

To achieve true wealth, it is essential to align your financial goals with your life purpose. This alignment ensures that your financial activities support your overall vision for a fulfilling and meaningful life.

- **Vision and Goals:** Clearly defining your long-term vision and setting specific, achievable financial goals that support this vision.

- **Personal Growth:** Continuously investing in your personal development and skills to adapt to changing circumstances and seize new opportunities.

- **Mindful Living:** Practicing mindfulness in financial decisions, ensuring that your actions are intentional and aligned with your values and purpose.

By adopting a revolutionary money mindset, you can transform your approach to wealth accumulation, embrace innovative financial strategies, and redefine success in a way that integrates material wealth with personal fulfillment and purpose. This holistic approach not only enhances your financial well-being but also contributes to a richer, more meaningful life.

Chapter 4: The Creator Economy

The digital revolution has given rise to a new economic paradigm known as the creator economy. This chapter delves into how digital platforms have democratized content creation and distribution, enabling individuals to turn their passions into profitable ventures. By exploring the rise of the creator economy, the opportunities it presents, and how to achieve financial independence through innovation, this chapter provides a comprehensive guide for aspiring digital entrepreneurs.

4.1 The Rise of the Creator Economy

How Digital Platforms are Changing the Game

The advent of digital platforms has fundamentally transformed how we create, share, and consume content. Platforms like YouTube, Instagram, TikTok, and Patreon have made it possible for individuals to reach global audiences with relative ease, bypassing traditional gatekeepers such as publishers and broadcasters.

- **Accessibility and Reach:** Digital platforms offer unprecedented access to a vast audience. Content creators can share their work instantly with millions of people worldwide.

- **Monetization Opportunities:** These platforms provide various monetization options, from ad revenue and sponsorships to direct fan contributions and subscription models.

- **Community Engagement:** Creators can interact directly with their audience, building a loyal community and receiving immediate feedback.

Opportunities in the Digital Age

The creator economy offers diverse opportunities for monetizing creativity. Whether you are a writer, musician, artist, or educator, there is a digital platform suited to your talents.

- **Content Creation:** Producing engaging content, such as videos, podcasts, blogs, and social media posts, can attract a large following and generate income through ads, sponsorships, and merchandise sales.

- **Digital Products:** Selling e-books, online courses, and digital art can provide a steady income stream with relatively low overhead costs.

- **Freelancing and Consulting:** Offering services such as graphic design, marketing, and web development through platforms like Fiverr and Upwork allows creators to monetize their skills.

4.2 Turning Passion into Profit

Leveraging Creativity for Financial Gain

Turning your passion into profit requires a strategic approach. It's not enough to be talented; you must also understand how to market and monetize your skills effectively.

- **Brand Building:** Establish a strong personal brand that reflects your unique voice and style. Consistent branding helps attract and retain followers.

- **Content Strategy:** Develop a content strategy that aligns with your audience's interests and needs. Regularly posting high-quality content increases engagement and loyalty.

- **Multiple Revenue Streams:** Diversify your income by exploring different monetization avenues, such as ads, sponsorships, product sales, and fan contributions.

Real-life Success Stories

Real-life success stories illustrate the potential of the creator economy. These individuals have leveraged their creativity and digital platforms to build thriving businesses:

- **PewDiePie:** Starting as a video game commentator on YouTube, Felix Kjellberg, known as PewDiePie, has amassed over 100 million subscribers and earned millions through ad revenue, sponsorships, and merchandise.

- **Pat Flynn:** An entrepreneur who transformed his blog and podcast, Smart Passive Income, into a multi-million-dollar business by sharing insights on online business and passive income strategies.

- **Huda Kattan:** A makeup artist who turned her beauty blog and YouTube channel, Huda Beauty, into a global cosmetics brand valued at over a billion dollars.

4.3 Achieving Financial Independence Through Innovation

Building a Sustainable Digital Business

Building a sustainable digital business in the creator economy involves more than just creating content. It requires innovation, strategic planning, and continuous learning.

- **Business Planning:** Treat your creative venture like a business. Develop a business plan that outlines your goals, target audience, monetization strategies, and growth plan.

- **Scalability:** Focus on creating scalable content and products that can reach a large audience without significantly increasing your workload.

- **Adaptability:** Stay abreast of industry trends and be willing to adapt your strategies to meet changing market demands and audience preferences.

Tools and Resources for Creators

A wide range of tools and resources can help creators streamline their workflow, improve content quality, and enhance audience engagement.

- **Content Creation Tools:** Software like Adobe Creative Cloud, Canva, and Final Cut Pro can enhance your content production capabilities.

- **Analytics Platforms:** Tools such as Google Analytics, YouTube Analytics, and Instagram Insights provide valuable data to understand audience behavior and optimize content strategies.

- **Monetization Platforms:** Patreon, Ko-fi, and Teachable enable creators to monetize their work through fan contributions, paid memberships, and online courses.

In summary, the creator economy offers immense potential for individuals to turn their passions into profitable, sustainable businesses. By leveraging digital platforms, adopting innovative strategies, and utilizing available tools, creators can achieve financial independence and thrive in the digital age.

Chapter 5: Secrets of Sustainable Wealth

Building sustainable wealth is more than just accumulating assets—it's about managing and preserving those assets over the long term and creating a legacy that benefits future generations. This chapter explores the principles of wealth building, effective management techniques, and strategies for ensuring long-term financial security.

5.1 Principles of Wealth Building

Foundations of Financial Growth

The foundation of sustainable wealth begins with understanding the key principles that drive financial growth. These principles are timeless and applicable regardless of the economic environment or personal circumstances.

- **Income Generation:** The first step in wealth building is generating income, whether through employment, business ventures, investments, or a combination of these. Diversifying income streams is crucial to mitigate risks and ensure steady financial growth.

- **Saving and Investing:** Consistently saving a portion of your income and investing it wisely is essential for wealth accumulation. This involves understanding various investment options, such as stocks, bonds, real estate, and mutual funds, and selecting those that align with your financial goals and risk tolerance.

- **Compound Interest:** Leveraging the power of compound interest can significantly accelerate wealth growth. Reinvesting earnings from investments leads to exponential growth over time.

Ethical Wealth Accumulation

Ethical wealth accumulation involves making financial decisions that align with your values and contribute positively to society. It's about earning and growing wealth in a way that does not exploit others or harm the environment.

- **Socially Responsible Investing (SRI):** Investing in companies and funds that prioritize ethical practices, such as environmental sustainability, fair labor practices, and corporate governance.

- **Philanthropy:** Incorporating charitable giving into your financial plan not only supports important causes but can also provide tax benefits.

- **Fair Business Practices:** Running businesses that adhere to ethical standards and contribute positively to the community and economy.

5.2 Maintaining Wealth Over the Long Term

Effective Wealth Management Techniques

Maintaining wealth requires strategic management to protect and grow your assets. Effective wealth management involves several key techniques:

- **Diversification:** Spreading investments across different asset classes and sectors to reduce risk. This includes a mix of equities, fixed income, real estate, and alternative investments.

- **Risk Management:** Identifying and mitigating financial risks through insurance, hedging, and maintaining an emergency fund. Proper risk management ensures that unexpected events do not derail your financial plan.

- **Regular Review and Adjustment:** Continuously monitoring your financial portfolio and making adjustments based on market conditions, personal goals, and risk tolerance. This proactive approach helps optimize returns and manage risks.

Strategies for Ethical Stewardship

Ethical stewardship involves managing your wealth in a way that aligns with your values and benefits society. This requires a long-term perspective and a commitment to responsible financial practices.

- **Impact Investing:** Investing in projects and companies that generate positive social and environmental impacts alongside financial returns. Examples include renewable energy projects and companies with strong social missions.

- **Sustainable Business Practices:** If you own a business, adopting sustainable practices that minimize environmental impact and promote social responsibility.

- **Community Engagement:** Using your resources to support and improve your community, whether through direct investment, philanthropy, or volunteerism.

5.3 Creating a Lasting Financial Legacy

Planning for Future Generations

Creating a lasting financial legacy involves planning not just for your own future, but for the well-being of your descendants. This requires careful estate planning and a focus on intergenerational wealth transfer.

- **Estate Planning:** Developing a comprehensive estate plan that includes wills, trusts, and beneficiary designations to ensure your assets are distributed according to your wishes. This also involves planning for potential estate taxes and other financial considerations.

- **Education and Mentorship:** Educating the next generation about financial management and investing principles. This includes providing formal education opportunities and informal mentorship to ensure they are equipped to manage the wealth they inherit.

- **Values-Based Legacy:** Communicating and instilling your values and principles in your heirs to ensure they continue to manage and use the wealth ethically and responsibly.

Systems for Ensuring Long-term Security

To ensure long-term financial security, it's important to establish systems and structures that protect and grow your wealth across generations.

- **Family Trusts:** Setting up family trusts can provide financial protection and management for future generations. Trusts can be structured to provide ongoing income, support education, and ensure that wealth is used in ways that align with your values.

- **Long-term Investment Strategies:** Adopting long-term investment strategies that focus on stability and growth, such as investing in blue-chip stocks, real estate, and other stable assets.

- **Regular Financial Reviews:** Conducting regular financial reviews with a financial advisor to ensure that your wealth management strategy remains aligned with your goals and adapts to changing circumstances.

In summary, building and maintaining sustainable wealth requires a strategic approach that balances financial growth with ethical considerations. By adhering to the principles of wealth building, implementing effective management techniques, and planning for future generations, you can create a financial legacy that provides lasting security and positive impact.

Chapter 6: Transformative Leadership and Change

Transformative leadership is crucial in shaping financial success and empowering others to achieve economic well-being. This chapter delves into the role of leadership in financial success, explores the concept of universal leadership and its impact on financial empowerment, and advocates for transformative change that aligns personal success with broader societal benefits.

6.1 The Role of Leadership in Financial Success

Guiding Yourself and Others

Leadership begins with guiding oneself effectively before extending influence to others. Successful financial leaders possess a deep understanding of their own financial goals and are capable of making informed decisions to achieve those goals.

- **Self-awareness:** Effective financial leaders possess a high level of self-awareness, understanding their strengths, weaknesses, and motivations. This self-awareness allows them to set realistic financial goals and develop strategies to achieve them.

- **Decision-making:** Sound decision-making skills are critical. Leaders need to evaluate financial opportunities and risks accurately and make decisions that align with their long-term objectives.

- **Resilience:** Financial leaders must be resilient, able to navigate setbacks and challenges without losing sight of their goals. This resilience fosters confidence and stability, which are crucial for long-term success.

Traits of Effective Financial Leaders

Effective financial leaders share certain traits that enable them to guide themselves and others towards financial success:

- **Vision:** They have a clear vision of what they want to achieve financially and can communicate this vision to others, inspiring them to work towards common goals.

- **Integrity:** Honesty and ethical behavior are foundational traits. Financial leaders act with integrity, earning the trust and respect of those they lead.

- **Empathy:** Understanding the needs and perspectives of others is crucial. Empathetic leaders can connect with their team or community on a deeper level, fostering a supportive environment.

- **Adaptability:** The financial landscape is constantly changing. Effective leaders are adaptable, able to pivot strategies and approaches as needed to stay on course.

- **Mentorship:** They prioritize mentorship, guiding others in their financial journeys and helping them develop the skills and knowledge necessary for success.

6.2 Universal Leadership and Financial Empowerment

The Purpose of Leadership

Universal leadership goes beyond personal financial success to encompass a broader purpose: empowering others and contributing to societal well-being. This type of leadership is characterized by a commitment to making a positive impact on the world.

- **Empowerment:** Universal leaders empower others by providing the tools, resources, and support needed to achieve financial independence. This includes education, mentorship, and access to opportunities.

- **Inclusion:** They advocate for inclusive financial practices, ensuring that diverse populations have the opportunity to participate in and benefit from the economy.

- **Service:** The purpose of leadership is fundamentally about service—serving others, the community, and the greater good.

Aligning Personal Success with Societal Benefits

True leadership aligns personal financial success with broader societal benefits. This means using one's financial success as a platform to drive positive change and improve the lives of others.

- **Corporate Social Responsibility (CSR):** Leaders in business can implement CSR initiatives that address social and environmental issues, creating a positive impact beyond their company's bottom line.

- **Philanthropy:** Personal financial success can be leveraged for philanthropic efforts, supporting causes and organizations that work towards societal betterment.

- **Advocacy:** Financial leaders can use their influence to advocate for policies and practices that promote economic justice, environmental sustainability, and social equity.

6.3 Advocating for Transformative Change

Financial Enlightenment as a Collective Goal

Financial enlightenment involves a collective shift in how we view and engage with money. This shift is necessary for achieving transformative change on a broader scale.

- **Education:** Promoting financial literacy and education is fundamental. When individuals understand how to manage their finances effectively, they are empowered to make better decisions and contribute to a healthier economy.

- **Awareness:** Raising awareness about the impact of financial practices on individuals, communities, and the environment is crucial. This includes understanding the consequences of consumerism, debt, and investment choices.

- **Collective Action:** Achieving financial enlightenment requires collective action. This means working together to create systems and structures that support financial well-being for all.

Implementing Change on a Broader Scale

Transformative change involves implementing strategies and policies that address systemic issues and promote financial well-being at a societal level.

- **Policy Advocacy:** Advocating for policies that support financial stability and growth for all individuals, such as affordable housing, access to education, and fair wages.

- **Community Initiatives:** Supporting community-based initiatives that promote financial empowerment, such as microfinance programs, small business support, and job training programs.

- **Sustainable Practices:** Encouraging businesses and individuals to adopt sustainable financial practices that consider long-term impacts on the environment and society.

Conclusion

Transformative leadership is essential for achieving financial success and empowering others. By guiding oneself and others, aligning personal success with societal benefits, and advocating for broader change, financial leaders can create a more inclusive and equitable economic landscape. The journey to financial enlightenment is a collective effort, and through education, awareness, and action, we can achieve lasting positive change.

Chapter 7: Inspiring Stories of Financial Empowerment

Around the world, individuals and organizations have harnessed the power of financial literacy, strategic investment, and innovative thinking to foster human development, personal growth, and wealth creation. Their stories serve as powerful examples of how the principles discussed in this book can be put into practice, transforming lives and communities. In this chapter, we explore the journeys of some of these remarkable people and organizations.

7.1 Mark Zuckerberg: Redefining Connectivity and Wealth

From Harvard Dorm Room to Global Influence

Mark Zuckerberg's journey began in a Harvard dorm room, where he and his friends created a platform that would eventually become Facebook. What started as a social networking site for college students transformed into a global phenomenon, connecting billions of people and creating unprecedented economic value.

Key Lessons

- **Vision and Innovation:** Zuckerberg's ability to envision a connected world and his relentless pursuit of innovation were critical to his success. He continually expanded Facebook's offerings, integrating new technologies and exploring new markets.

- **Scaling for Impact:** By focusing on scalability, Zuckerberg ensured that Facebook's impact would be global. This approach not only maximized financial returns but also extended the platform's social influence.

- **Philanthropy:** Zuckerberg and his wife, Priscilla Chan, have committed significant portions of their wealth to philanthropic efforts, particularly in education and healthcare, demonstrating a commitment to leveraging financial success for societal benefit.

7.2 Jeff Bezos: Revolutionizing E-commerce and Beyond

The Amazon Empire

Jeff Bezos founded Amazon in 1994 as an online bookstore, but his vision extended far beyond books. He transformed Amazon into the largest e-commerce platform in the world, diversifying into various sectors including cloud computing, entertainment, and artificial intelligence.

Key Lessons

- **Customer-Centric Approach:** Bezos' obsessive focus on customer satisfaction drove Amazon's growth. By prioritizing customer needs, Amazon built a loyal customer base and achieved market dominance.

- **Long-Term Thinking:** Bezos' willingness to reinvest profits into new ventures and his patience for long-term growth have been crucial. This long-term approach allowed Amazon to innovate continuously and stay ahead of competitors.

- **Wealth Creation and Philanthropy:** Bezos has used his wealth to invest in space exploration through Blue Origin and contribute to climate change mitigation efforts, showing how financial success can be channeled towards ambitious, transformative projects.

7.3 Peter Thiel: From PayPal to Pioneering Investments

Building and Investing in the Future

Peter Thiel co-founded PayPal, which revolutionized online payments. After selling PayPal, he became a prominent venture capitalist, investing in groundbreaking companies like Facebook and Palantir Technologies.

Key Lessons

- **Identifying Disruptive Innovation:** Thiel's success lies in his ability to identify and invest in companies with the potential to disrupt industries and create new markets.

- **Contrarian Thinking:** Thiel advocates for thinking differently and challenging conventional wisdom. His contrarian approach has led him to invest in and support ventures that others might overlook.

- **Philanthropy and Advocacy:** Thiel supports initiatives that promote technological progress and innovation, such as the Thiel Fellowship, which encourages young people to pursue ambitious projects instead of traditional educational paths.

7.4 Ijigban Daniel Oketa: Innovating for a Better World

Overcoming Financial Barriers

As an entrepreneur, Ijigban Daniel Oketa faced significant challenges due to lack of access to finance for testing ideas or scaling businesses. During these trying times, he discovered the intrinsic value of money as a tool for personal development and wealth creation aimed at contributing to human evolution for a better world.

Key Lessons

- **Innovation Amidst Adversity:** Despite financial constraints, Oketa continued to innovate and develop his ideas, demonstrating that perseverance and creativity can overcome financial barriers.

- **Intrinsic Value of Money:** Oketa learned to view money not just as a means to an end, but as a tool for achieving personal growth and contributing positively to society.

- **Spreading Knowledge:** Today, Oketa is dedicated to using money the right way, contributing to human development and evolution through the spread of H-TIPS (Human and Time Innovation Power System). This revolutionary principle and system focuses on personal growth and development, transformative leadership, and promoting peace and unity. Oketa's work helps individuals fulfill their leadership potential and work towards a sustainable world devoid of evil.

7.5 The Grameen Bank: Microfinance for Economic Empowerment

Empowering the Poor through Microcredit

Founded by Nobel laureate Muhammad Yunus, the Grameen Bank provides microloans to the poor in Bangladesh, empowering them to start small businesses and achieve financial independence.

Key Lessons

- **Financial Inclusion:** By providing access to credit for those traditionally excluded from the financial system, Grameen Bank has helped millions lift themselves out of poverty.

- **Sustainable Development:** The bank's focus on sustainable, community-driven development demonstrates how financial services can drive long-term economic growth and social progress.

- **Social Impact:** The success of Grameen Bank has inspired microfinance initiatives worldwide, highlighting the potential for financial innovation to create widespread social impact.

7.6 Financial Literacy Programs: Educating for Empowerment

Improving Financial Literacy Globally

Organizations like Junior Achievement and the National Endowment for Financial Education (NEFE) are dedicated to improving financial literacy worldwide. They provide educational programs that teach essential financial skills to children and adults.

Key Lessons

- **Early Education:** Teaching financial literacy from a young age helps individuals develop healthy financial habits that last a lifetime.

- **Community Engagement:** These programs often involve community engagement, ensuring that financial education is accessible to diverse populations.

- **Empowerment through Knowledge:** By equipping people with the knowledge they need to manage their finances effectively, these programs empower individuals to make informed financial decisions and achieve economic security.

7.7 Oprah Winfrey: Using Wealth for Empowerment and Influence

From Poverty to Media Mogul

Oprah Winfrey's rise from poverty to becoming one of the most influential media moguls in the world is a testament to the power of resilience, hard work, and strategic financial decisions.

Key Lessons

- **Personal Branding:** Oprah's ability to build a powerful personal brand has been central to her financial success. Her authenticity and connection with her audience have driven her media empire.

- **Diverse Investments:** Beyond media, Oprah has invested in various sectors, including education and health, leveraging her wealth to create broader social impact.

- **Philanthropy:** Oprah's philanthropic efforts, particularly in education, exemplify how personal success can be used to empower others and drive positive change.

Conclusion

These stories of individuals and organizations around the world illustrate the diverse paths to financial empowerment and the profound impact that strategic financial decisions can have on personal and societal well-being. From tech moguls like Mark Zuckerberg and Jeff Bezos to pioneers of financial inclusion like Muhammad Yunus, and innovative thinkers like Ijigban Daniel Oketa, these examples demonstrate that understanding the psychology of money, embracing innovation, and committing to ethical principles can lead to remarkable success and lasting positive change.

Conclusion: Embracing Comprehensive Financial and Personal Growth

In the journey through "The Psychology of Money, Growth, and Wealth," we have explored the intricate interplay between financial decisions, personal beliefs, and societal impact. This exploration has revealed that money is far more than a medium of exchange; it embodies our values, aspirations, and the potential for profound transformation. As we conclude this journey, it becomes clear that integrating spiritual insight, practical advice, and psychological acumen is essential to redefining our relationship with money and achieving comprehensive financial and personal growth.

Integrating Spiritual Insight

Throughout this book, we have emphasized the spiritual dimension of money—the notion that our financial behaviors are deeply rooted in our inner values and spiritual beliefs. Understanding this connection allows us to align our financial goals with our broader life purpose, ensuring that our pursuit of wealth is not merely materialistic but also enriching to our spiritual well-being. By viewing money as a force for good, we can channel our resources towards endeavors that promote human flourishing and societal harmony.

Practical Advice for Financial Empowerment

Practical advice has been a cornerstone of our exploration, addressing common money mistakes, promoting financial awareness, and advocating for innovative financial strategies. We have discussed the importance of understanding the true value of money beyond its superficial allure, and the pitfalls of consumerism that can hinder our path to financial security. By fostering mindfulness in spending and saving, and adopting transformative financial strategies, we empower ourselves to navigate economic challenges with resilience and foresight.

Psychological Acumen for Personal Growth

Psychological insights have illuminated how our attitudes towards money shape our financial outcomes. From the revolutionary mindset needed for wealth accumulation to the transformative leadership required for societal change, we have examined how our beliefs and behaviors influence not only our personal financial success but also our ability to positively impact the world around us. By embracing a growth mindset and cultivating emotional intelligence in financial decision-making, we position ourselves for lasting personal growth and fulfillment.

The Path to Redefining Your Relationship with Money

Redefining your relationship with money begins with introspection and a willingness to explore its spiritual, practical, and psychological dimensions. It involves questioning conventional wisdom, challenging societal norms, and embracing innovation in pursuit of financial and personal goals. By leveraging the principles discussed in this book—such as ethical wealth accumulation, sustainable investment practices, and inclusive financial literacy—we forge a path towards financial independence that aligns with our values and aspirations.

Achieving Comprehensive Financial and Personal Growth

Comprehensive financial and personal growth is not solely about accumulating wealth, but also about leveraging our resources to create meaningful impact in our lives and communities. It is about stewardship—managing our finances ethically and responsibly to ensure long-term security and prosperity. By integrating spiritual insight, practical advice, and psychological acumen, we empower ourselves to lead purposeful lives driven by financial wisdom, personal fulfillment, and a commitment to contribute positively to the world.

As you reflect on the insights gained from "The Psychology of Money, Growth, and Wealth," may you embark on a journey of continuous learning and growth, transforming your relationship with money into a catalyst for profound personal and societal change. Embrace the opportunities ahead with clarity, courage, and compassion, knowing that your journey towards comprehensive financial and personal growth is both empowering and transformative.

Congratulations!

Ijigban Daniel Oketa

About the Book

The Psychology of Money, Growth, and Wealth" delves deep into the complex interplay between our psychological attitudes, spiritual beliefs, and financial behaviors.

This enlightening exploration not only unravels the essence of money as a tool for personal development and societal impact but also offers practical guidance on navigating the modern financial landscape.

Through a blend of spiritual insight, practical advice, and psychological acumen, this book challenges readers to redefine their relationship with money, fostering comprehensive financial growth and personal fulfillment.

Discover transformative strategies that empower individuals to align their financial goals with their deepest values, paving the way for a more prosperous and purpose-driven life.

Ijigban Daniel Oketa

Ijigban Daniel Oketa offers a personal journey through the challenges of entrepreneurship and financial limitations, emphasizing the transformative power of innovation and the intrinsic value of money.

His narrative unfolds as a testament to resilience and growth, illustrating how his creation and implementation of H-TIPS (Human and Time Innovation Power System) revolutionized personal development, transformative leadership, and societal change.

Through this book, Oketa shares profound insights and practical strategies, aiming to inspire readers to harness the potential of money for positive human evolution and sustainable global impact.

You can know more about Mr. Oketa by visiting www.idoketa.com
Telephone: +234 703-738-4814
oketadaniels@gmail.com

www.ingramcontent.com/pod-product-compliance
Lightning Source LLC
Chambersburg PA
CBHW072001210526
45479CB00003B/1023